To:

From:

"embrace thy clutter!"

Published by
The CreativeCabin
PITTSBURGH, PA USA

Copyright 2012

ALL RIGHTS RESERVED

INCLUDING THE RIGHT OF REPRODUCTION

IN WHOLE OR IN PART IN ANY FORM.

PRINTED IN THE USA

fengshlop.com

MAKE LIFE EASY!

The realistic approach

to balancing life, love, work, family,

and all the 'shlop' that

goes along with it.

relax

IMAGINE

You're not perfect...

MAKE LIFE EASY!

but you're perfectly fine...

just the way you are!

relax

it's

to want to improve your life...

great!

MAKE LIFE EASY!

Feng Shui [fēng shǔi]
Achieve harmony with your environment.

relax

It's ok to let some things go.

MAKE LIFE EASY!

Feng Shlop [fēng shlop]

Embrace life realistically!

... while creatively loafing!

MAKE LIFE EASY!

Nurture Your Natural.

relax

Acceptance

"I can't find the corners of my rooms at home!

It's so challenging
to juggle 40 hours of office time
with schedules
and family demands."

~ Mother, Accountant

MAKE LIFE EASY!

Feng Shlop is about Acceptance

Accepting life as it really is and people as they really are.

You don't have to learn a lot of complicated principles and rules of energy to find renewal.

You simply have to

tap into the energy zones

YOU
already have!

relax

We all
know
that
fighting
"what if"
zaps our
energy…

MAKE LIFE EASY!

For example, if we wrestle our kindergartner into early morning school clothes ~ we don't seem to win anyway. 'Fighting' at work over an unreasonable demand is exhausting.

If we accept that we should ease into the day, (grade schoolers do look fabulous in unmatched outfits), we maintain our energy and enjoy the day, our kids and our work more.

What's more, we have the energy we need for the battles that really count.

relax

tap into
what we
all
already
have

Acceptance allows energy to grow and expand.

MAKE LIFE EASY!

Acceptance gives you room to breathe.
It allows you to discover ways to increase your energy naturally.

Increase your energy by allowing yourself to:
Appreciate the 'stink bug' that is enjoying your basil plant.

Slow down,
chew and really taste the food you eat, you may even eat less and lose weight!

Go for a bike ride or a walk.   Take a spinning class ... Ride a sit-n-spin!

Sit in nature.
Enjoy an ice cold glass of water, plus or minus lime ... lemons ...

Enjoy a meal without jumping up to serve your kids or guests.

Enjoy a glass of wine.

Nourish your body with a healthy meal.

Indulge in a nap!

MAKE LIFE EASY!

Blunder til you balance.

relax

24
hours
1440
minutes
88,400
seconds

just
be

MAKE LIFE EASY!

**No matter how you slice it,
you get 24 hours every day…
… no more, no less.**

The temptation is to fill those hours

until they overflow, with work and stuff,

work and stuff

and more work and 'shtuff'.

relax

What's your OK imperfection?

add photo here

to appreciate later

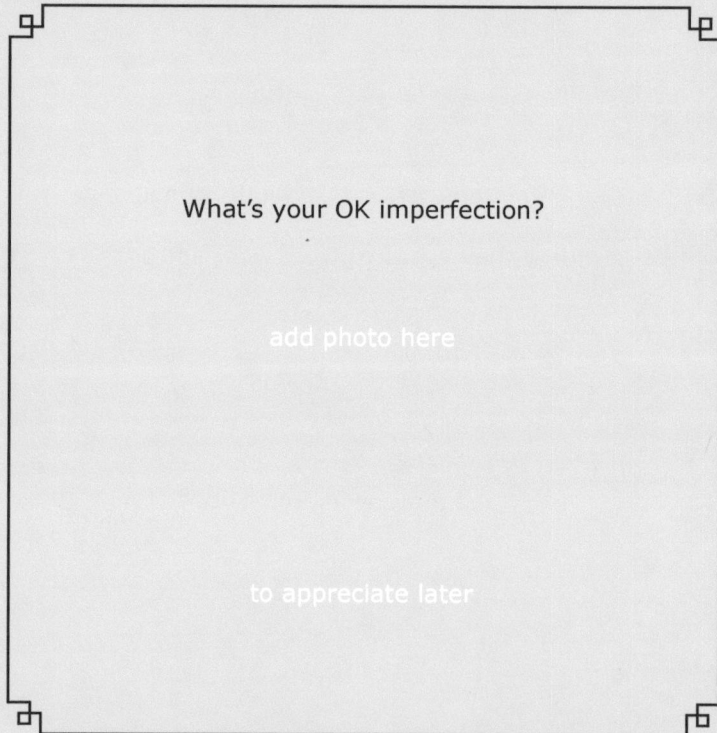

MAKE LIFE EASY!

Yet, no matter how many hours you put into your stuff …

…your work, your home,

and the other things you maintain,

they will <u>never</u> be perfect.

You'll never get it all exactly right, embrace that reality.

The **principle of balance** with Feng Shlop encourages you to give your work an appropriate block of time

and then **let it go**.

relax

too much shtuff
shop

make time for emotional organizing

MAKE LIFE EASY!

**Strive for excellence where it counts,
and bid unrealistic perfectionism farewell, forever.
Balance demands good time management skills*.**

After all, we all carry the demands of work and life's mundane chores.

Make a plan for the things you must do.

Keep yourself organized and stay on top of things, more or less.

Choose activities that give you energy, and luxuriate in these things.

Feed your values and support the important priorities in your life.

It's okay to give in to urges and creative impulses

as long as the basics are kept in order.

This is blundering til you balance!

relax

your
day will go
the way
the corners
of your
mouth
turn

MAKE LIFE EASY!

Decide why you believe you are on the earth and live that mission.

Make time in every week to align your time with what you believe is important.

If you believe in prayer, make time for it.
If you believe in building houses for the poor,
schedule that activity into your calendar.

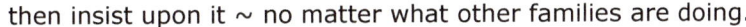

If you believe in families eating dinner together,

then insist upon it ~ no matter what other families are doing.

relax

accept

spont-
a-
neity

Banish excess ... see real treasures!

MAKE LIFE EASY!

Feng Shlop calls you to notice the natural ways you want to relax ~
the things that balance out the urge to perfectionism.

Feng Shlop reminds you to be 'structured enough',
because that's the only way to fulfill the demands of life.

But structure and rigidity are not synonyms.

Accept spontaneity and opportunity in life.

The Feng Shlop way is to feed your family good, nutritious food
and top it off with an occasional double scoop of ice cream.

Occasional being key here ...

relax

MAKE LIFE EASY!

Loaf
creatively
!

relax

this is easy!

hmmmmmm

let's
'relax' ....

unplug!
electronics

MAKE LIFE EASY!

We live in a culture where the word "relax"

is something you do a couple times a year.

Hmmmm ... let's 'relax' ...

Many think ushering an entire family onto an airplane
and paying enormous ticket prices to "do" a theme park is relaxing?
When you get home, your wallet is empty,
your kids are cranky from the travel, and you are exhausted.

Similar relaxation happens with all the emphasis on *organized* sports and activities.

Whatever happened to spontaneity,

like catching fireflies in recyclable jars?

Feng Shlop advises you to embrace loafing frequently, creatively, and affordably.
Forget the fancy, high-priced destination vacations and go on a picnic.
Save the fancy, high-priced destination vacations for just you and a 'date'. *or*

Save the fancy, high-priced destination vacation

for just **YOU**!

relax

hey
here's an
idea!

MAKE LIFE EASY!

Look for ways to break out of the pattern of your every day routine.

Look for an auction … or a new B&B.

Research what's available within an hour or two's drive from your home.

Pile the kids, or friends, in the car and head out on adventure.

You will have to use your creativity
to find time to loaf
as much as you'll need to use your creativity
to mix up your approaches to loafing.

With pressure to fill schedules,
it takes organization as well as commitment
to fit in a regular measure of loafing.

Give yourself permission to loaf and then flaunt it to your neighbors.
They won't know what to think!
Leave your technology unattended
and the whole world will think you've lost your mind.

relax

break out
of your
patterns

find
fun!

MAKE LIFE EASY!

just a few ideas...

Camp at lake.
Book an overnite or two at that resort you see advertised.
Doodle & draw.

Travel to an exotic place on that watercolor weekend retreat ...
Build a sandcastle, visit a castle ....
Go out to dinner, open a Diner.   Visit a pet shop, adopt a pet.

Cut coupons, toss the coupons you have cluttering up your purse!
Read a cooking magazine, hire a caterer for your next pool party.

Build a bonfire, make S'mores.
Host an indoor picnic on a rainy day. Prepare a meal as a family.

Window shop, shop for Windows ...
Write in a journal ~ publish a book!
Tell family stories ~ make new family memories.
Volunteer at a soup kitchen. Donate to a soup kitchen ...

Take a nap ...
Read a book ... Book a Cruise.

Do nothing at all.
Period

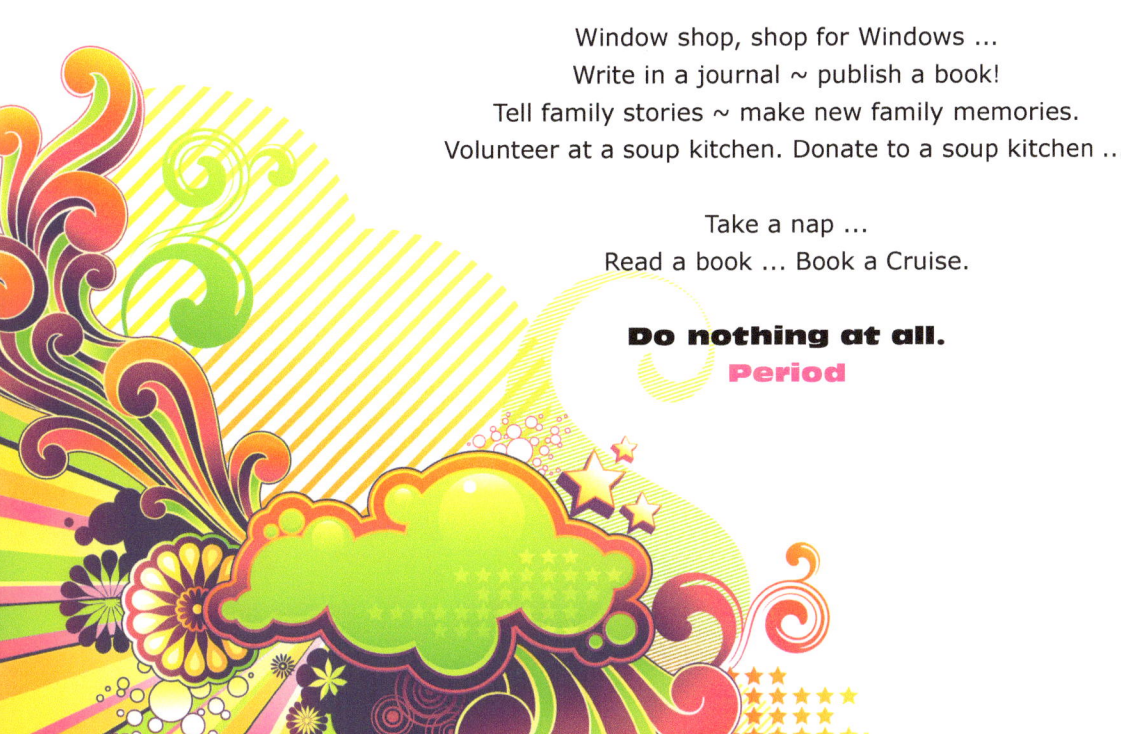

relax

focus on the parts of life you get right

B Gentle with yourself.

Be curator of your stuff ... display only the most loved.

relax

Pick out the gems of your 'shtuff' and let go of the rest.

MAKE LIFE EASY!

Okay,
so we all need a certain amount of order.

Give yourself permission to structure your space and your time efficiently.
Hire a professional organizer if that will help you to get the basics down.
(or just ask a friend, an honest one)

A good organizer can help you understand how you think
and help you to structure your space in a way you can manage.

Then, give yourself permission to focus on the parts of life you get right.
Notice the spaces you keep in order
rather than obsess on the ones that tend to get out of hand.

MAKE LIFE EASY!

When you pursue perfection, you spend your energy on negatives:
shame, blame, guilt, and all that shtuff. Who needs it?!

These negatives will suck the energy right out of you.

The Feng Shlop way is to accept and embrace that place you find yourself in.
Negative thoughts are a form of self-poisoning.
If your thoughts are consistently in a negative zone, your health will go there too.
Your relationships will be soured and tainted.

relax

Embrace the

person

you are.

MAKE LIFE EASY!

If you spend your time rehearsing negative moments from your past,
those moments will have enduring power to spoil your current moments.

Why not rehearse the happy memories,
even if they are fewer than the not-so-happy ones?

Fighting the past is a useless struggle.

You'll never win.
Embrace the person you are, and control what you can control in the present moment.
If you are short of happy memories in the past, create some new memories today.
Embrace today and the people with whom you share your life.
Then you'll have happy memories for tomorrow.

Kids, spouses, parents, friends and pets all have annoying stages and habits.
Have you noticed this?
Have you noticed how even YOU annoy YOURSELF sometimes?!
Not to mention the kids, spouses,
parents, friends and pets **you** annoy??

MAKE LIFE EASY!

On the other hand, have you noticed the twinkle
in a child's eye when you express your pride in their accomplishment?

Have you noticed what it means to a parent when you offer a
hug or a word of thanks?

Life is fleeting.

Don't waste it with negative people and friends.

Find things to appreciate in each phase of life with your children, yourself, your friends.

Take a photo of the hamper and put it in your album

(or that messy box of photos you've been meaning to put in an album)

so you can look back and remember that

you

valued the important things in life.

relax

important shtuff!

Keep your possessions and treasures to scale

~ so they do not burden you,

ultimate goal of curating your shtuff!

MAKE LIFE EASY!

my photo example of
proof that I value something important

relax

When you can let go, it proves you are more

than the sum of your material possessions.

Embrace thy clutter

MAKE LIFE EASY!

Feed Your Spirit
too.

simple philosophy

MAKE LIFE EASY!

Your spirit is your life force that connects with a higher Power in some way.

It's the part of you that stretches beyond this physical world and searches for meaning.

No matter what your religious beliefs, feed the needs of your spirit.

Don't allow the demands of work, parenthood,
or any other duty crowd out this essential part of yourself.

You can only achieve a sense of well-being
if you regularly feed your spirit.

relax

do something 'real'

MAKE LIFE EASY!

Is there a part of you that aches to make a contribution ~
to participate in making this world a better place?

That's your spirit.

Learn more about spirit by taking time
to clarify your mission in life.
Once you have clarity,
align your daily life to match your mission.

If you don't live up to your mission every day, however,
avoid beating yourself up over it.

It's okay.

Do the best you can and accept your limitations.

Spend time with people who share your spiritual values.

Limit the time you spend with people who draw you away from your values.

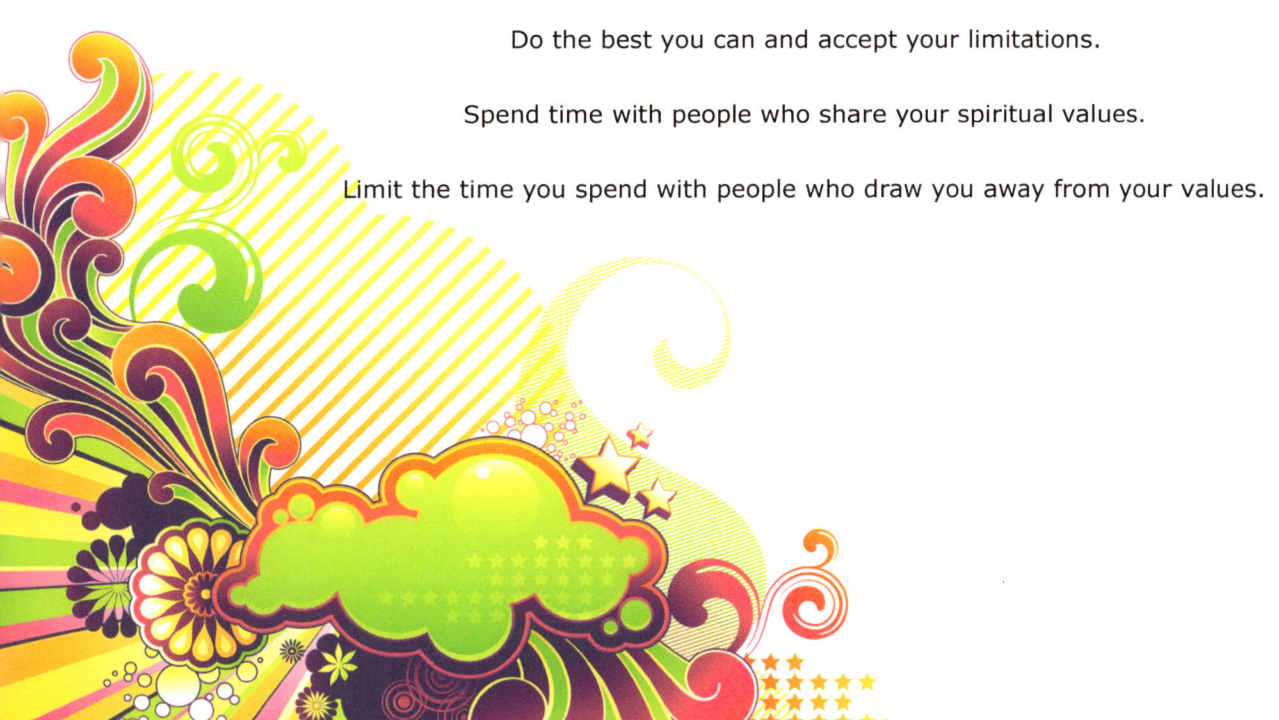

relax

it's okay

Gratitude naturally lifts your spirit.

MAKE LIFE EASY!

Consider the following simple activities that have power to renew your spirit:

Meditate
Walk in nature
Read
Attend services
Breathe
Drink water
Listen to your higher power
Cultivate periods of solitude
Tend a garden

One sure way to feed your spirit is to live a life of appreciation and gratitude.

When you focus on aspects of your life that you appreciate,
your sense of well-being grows.
When you express appreciation to the people who bless your life,
your relationships get richer.

Gratitude naturally lifts your spirit.
It also makes you aware that you are very fortunate.
Find a way to contribute, to give back, to bless others.
The very act of giving will renew your energy source.

relax

Breathe!

MAKE LIFE EASY!

Fill Life with Laughing.

Let Relief wash over you.

Keep your possessions and treasures and momentos to scale.

A life that fits is its own reward,
no one is perfect and it's perfectly fine to embrace just that.

Embrace Feng Shlop.

relax

hey
here's an
idea! ANOTHER

MAKE LIFE EASY!

no expiration date

Give a Gift of Presence
Your time

versus a present, aka more Shlop to deal with.

This coupon entitles recipient to:

(check one or more)

❏ **a walk**

❏ **lunch**

❏ **a drive to an appointment**

❏ **tea**

❏ **conversation**

❏ _____

You Are Beauty Full!

MAKE LIFE EASY!

Give YOURSELF

a Gift of: 'It's OK

Embrace Thy Clutter'

Take time off from all of what probably does not really matter too much anyway.

no expiration date

relax

MAKE LIFE EASY!

www.ingramcontent.com/pod-product-compliance
Lightning Source LLC
LaVergne TN
LVHW072125070426
835512LV00002B/16